Developing Literacy
SPEAKING & LISTENING

PHOTOCOPIABLE ACTIVITIES
FOR THE LITERACY HOUR

year

Ray Barker and
Christine Moorcroft

Contents

Drama

Acknowledgements

The authors and publishers are grateful for permission to reproduce extracts from the following:
p. 16 *The Amazing Adventures of Soupy Boy* by Damon Burnard, published by Corgi Yearling. Reprinted by permission of
The Random House Group Ltd; p. 17 *Mr Croc Rocks* copyright © 1999 Frank Rodgers, reproduced by kind permission of Frank Rodgers
c/o Caroline Sheldon Literary Agency Limited; p. 44 'Magic Cat' by Peter Dixon, from *Peter Dixon's Grand Prix of Poetry* by Peter Dixon
(copyright © 1999 Macmillan Publishers Limited). Every effort has been made to trace copyright holders and to obtain their permission for use
of copyright material. The authors and publishers would be pleased to rectify in future editions any error or omission.

Published 2006 by A & C Black Publishers Limited
38 Soho Square, London W1D 3HB
www.acblack.com

ISBN-10: 0-7136-7372-9
ISBN-13: 978-0-7136-7372-2

Copyright text © Ray Barker, 2006
Copyright illustrations © David Benham, 2006
Copyright cover illustration © Andy Robb, 2006
Editors: Lynne Williamson and Marie Lister
Designer: Heather Billin

The authors and publishers would like to thank Fleur Lawrence and Rifat Siddiqui for their advice in producing this series of books.
A CIP catalogue record for this book is available from the British Library.

Printed and bound in Great Britain by Cromwell Press Ltd, Trowbridge, Wiltshire.

A & C Black uses paper produced with elemental chlorine-free pulp, harvested from managed sustainable forests.

Introduction

Developing Literacy: Speaking and Listening is a series of seven photocopiable activity books for the Literacy Hour. Each book provides a range of speaking and listening activities and supports the teaching and learning objectives identified in *Curriculum Guidance for the Foundation Stage* and by the Primary National Strategy in *Speaking, Listening, Learning: working with children in Key Stages 1 and 2.*

Speaking and listening skills are vital to children's intellectual and social development, particularly in helping them to:

- develop creativity;
- interact with others;
- solve problems;
- speculate and discourse;
- form social relationships;
- build self-confidence.

The activities in this book focus on the following four aspects of speaking and listening:

- **Speaking:** being able to speak clearly; developing and sustaining ideas in talk
- **Listening:** developing active listening strategies; using skills of analysis
- **Group discussion and interaction:** taking different roles in groups; working collaboratively; making a range of contributions
- **Drama:** improvisation; working in role; scripting and performing; responding to performances

Using the activity sheets

The materials show how speaking and listening can be relevant to all parts of literacy lessons, in whole-class work, in group or paired work, during independent work and in plenary sessions. The activities encourage the inclusion of all learners, since talking and contributing to group work are often more accessible than writing for lower-achieving children and for those who speak English as an additional language.

Extension activities

Most of the activity sheets end with a challenge (**Now try this!**), which reinforces and extends the children's learning and provides the teacher with an opportunity for assessment. These more challenging activities might be appropriate for only a few children; it is not expected that the whole class should complete them. For most of the extension activities, the children will need a notebook or a separate sheet of paper.

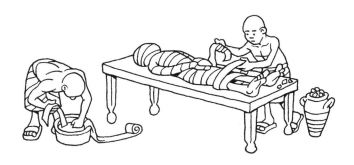

Organisation

Few resources are needed besides scissors, glue, word banks and simple dictionaries. Access to ICT resources – computers, videos, tape recorders – will also be useful at times. To help teachers select appropriate learning experiences for their pupils, the activities are grouped into sections within the book. The pages need not be presented in the order in which they appear, unless stated otherwise. The sheets are intended to support, rather than direct, the teacher's planning.

Brief notes are provided at the bottom of each page, giving ideas and suggestions for making the most of the activity sheet. They may include suggestions for a whole-class introduction, a plenary session or follow-up work. These notes may be masked before photocopying if desired. More detailed notes and suggestions can be found on pages 6–8.

Effective group work

Many of the activities involve children working in groups. Here are some ideas to consider as you prepare for group work.

Before you start

HOW?

- How are deadlines and groupings made clear to groups?
- How might different children undertake different tasks?
- How will you organise time and space to give children the opportunity to rehearse and practise new skills?
- How will the children reflect on what they have learned about talk and its impact?

WHEN?

- When is working in a group appropriate?
- When is speaking and listening the focus of an activity?
- When is speaking and listening the outcome?
- When is it right for one child to become 'an expert' and inform others?

WHERE?

- Where in the class is the work going to take place in order to give space and manage noise levels?
- Where is it best for you to be to monitor the groups?
- Where might group work result in a finished product, such as a leaflet, and what resources will you need?

Tips for grouping children

- Be clear about the nature and purpose of the task.
- Decide which type of grouping is best for your purpose (pairs, attainment groups, friendship groups).
- Consider the advantages of mixed- or single-sex groupings in your particular class.
- Consider how you will include all abilities in these groups.
- Think carefully about who will lead groups and how you can vary this.
- Aim to vary the experience for the children: for example, using different groupings, ways of recording or learning environments. Experiment with what works best for different kinds of learners.

Your role

The notes in this book suggest an active role for you as a teacher, and give examples of how you can develop children's learning. Your role will vary from activity to activity, but here are some general points to bear in mind when working with children on speaking and listening activities:

- Be challenging in your choice of topics.
- Do not be afraid to use the correct language for talk: for example, *dialogue, gesture, narrator, negotiate, open and closed questions* and so on.
- Set the ground rules: everyone has a right to speak but everyone also has a duty to listen to others, take turns and so on.
- Move around to monitor what is happening in the groups. You can move on group discussions by developing and questioning what the children say.
- Provide models of the patterns of language expected for particular kinds of speech.
- Try to steer children away from using closed questions.
- Ensure children give extended answers and always ask them to explain their thinking.
- Allow children time to formulate their responses and treat everyone's responses with respect – but avoid praising every answer.

Assessment

An assessment sheet is provided on page 48 for children to assess their own progress. The children can complete the sheet on their own or in discussion with you. It is not expected that you will be able to assess the entire class at any one time. It is best to focus on a small group of children each week, although whole-class monitoring may be possible with certain activities, such as drama activities where children perform to the whole class.

Other activities in the book are ideal for the collection of evidence over the year (for example, *School dinner discussions, Food chains, All about kittens, Plastic fun, Add an adjective, Speech success: 1 and 2*) and for children to assess one another's skills in speaking and listening (for example, *School dinner arguments, Story maker, Good evening… and welcome, Bright ideas, Speech success: 2*). All the information should be assimilated for an end-of-year summary to facilitate target setting and the transition to Year 5.

Notes on the activities

Speaking

The activities in this section provide contexts to encourage the children to speak clearly, audibly and with control to a partner, another adult, their group or the class and to be aware of their audience.

Dog rules – OK! (page 9). For this activity the children should bear in mind ground rules for dialogue, such as taking turns to speak and respecting others' contributions. After they have devised their own 'pet' rules and have talked about any problems encountered, discuss what further rules might be necessary for group work. Ask the children to reflect on what happened during their own group work.

Animal sort: 1 and 2 (pages 10–11). Here the children should work as a group, to listen to each other's contributions and to come to conclusions about how the animals are similar and different. Ensure that all children in the group get a turn to speak and make a contribution.

School dinner discussions (page 12). Stress that a discussion involves people getting together and talking about issues – not thinking that there is a 'right answer' or that they must convince someone of their views. Help the children to complete their answers and encourage them to sequence their views, asking questions such as: 'Which are the most important?' 'Which ones follow on logically?'

School dinner arguments (page 13). Encourage the children to come up with arguments and also reasons for them. Talk about advertising (see pages 30 and 35) and the use of persuasive language. In the extension activity, the children role-play an argument where they give their views persuasively. You could ask them to use different scenarios to explore how aspects of the role-play would change: for example, a debate in parliament or an argument in the playground.

Mapping journeys (page 14). Read the six statements about the early life of Jesus and ask the children what they know about these stories. They could look in the Bible to check their understanding of the events. The activity could be carried out with source material relating to other journeys in the context of RE, history or geography.

Story maker (page 15). At first the children's stories will no doubt be quite typical in storyline and characterisation. Each child should respond to the wild card chosen for them by considering how this element might affect their story. Encourage the children to share ideas and to discuss the new direction of the story: for example, what happens to a traditional fairy tale when a computer is introduced? What kind of story might this now become?

Soupy Boy (page 16). It is important to set the learning objective clearly before the children tell their stories and are assessed. The main focus should be on the way the story is told, using the voice effectively to interest the audience and convey the message. You could also incorporate other objectives, such as how stories are structured. You may wish to create an assessment form for the children to complete (similar to the one on page 40).

Cartoon crazy (page 17). Provide the class with some assessment points so that the children can give feedback on one another's stories: for example, was the speaking clear? Was it structured? How did body language help? How did the speaker use his or her voice to make the story interesting? If you do not want the children to cut out the pieces, you could add letters and ask the children to list the correct order.

Food chains (page 18). In this activity the children should concentrate on using their voices effectively. The activity sheet gives information about a food chain in visual and note form and asks the children to explain the process. Discuss features such as: presenting the ideas in a logical order; not expecting an audience to understand technical language; and what kind of connectives will be useful to link the four stages. Talk about different ways of using the voice to hold an audience's interest: for example, speaking expressively and varying the pace and volume.

Listening

These activities develop children's skills as active listeners and help them to join in meaningful discussions. Remind them what it means to be a good listener: for example, looking at the speaker and not fidgeting.

Good evening... and welcome (page 19). You could start by watching a television presenter interviewing a celebrity and noting the kinds of questions he or she asks, and the tone of voice used. The speech bubbles on the activity sheet contain clues as to their logical order: for example, the first question asked is usually an easy one to make the person feel comfortable; the following ones use language which suggests sequence, such as *first* and *next*. Discuss with the children how the tone of voice can change the meaning of what is said. Talk about tones of voice which are appropriate in different situations: for example, it would not be appropriate for a television presenter to lose his or her temper on screen.

How does it make you feel? (page 20). Initially when you play the video to the children, ask them to focus on the music rather than the images on screen. When they have commented on the music, begin to consider the images and how they add to the effect: for example, are they cartoon-like which may suggest comedy? Are the colours bright or dark, and what mood does this create? What is happening in the images? Is there any text on screen and how does it appear?

Television sight and sound (page 21). Here the children focus on the presentational features used to communicate the main points in an information programme. Ask the children what they learn from the images they see and the sounds they hear, and what effect is created. For the extension activity, the children will need to watch the extracts again with the sound turned off.

Take pride (page 22). Before the children start the activity, show extracts from television documentaries. Compare the narrators' voices and discuss how their way of speaking contributes to the overall tone of the programme. Encourage the children to experiment with saying the same words in different ways to create different effects with their voices.

Getting stressed (page 23). This activity could be extended into role-play activities. Using the sentence in the extension activity, ask the children to think of different situations in which the sentence could be used and what the circumstances could be.

All about kittens (page 24). Read aloud the following passage to the children and ask them to make notes:

Looking after a kitten

A kitten should be at least eight weeks old before it is taken away from its mother. A healthy kitten is very curious, so when choosing a kitten, look for one which is playful. As a kitten's stomach is so small – no larger than your thumbnail when it is born – it needs to eat many small meals packed with nutrients. A kitten's eye colour will change. You will not find out the true colour of your cat's eyes until it is one year old. A kitten's weight increases 40–50 times by the time it is fully grown.

Plastic fun (page 25). Here the children listen to a talk by a partner and make notes which they then use to draw the object being described. There may be different ways of making the objects; encourage the children to discuss whether one another's suggestions are possible.

Phone a friend (page 26). Discuss how certain kinds of talk 'open' a conversation and other kinds 'close' it. This links with the kinds of questions used in interviews (see page 42). Ask: 'How old do you think the speaker is? Is the speaker male or female? Why do you think this?'

Hello, goodbye (page 27). At the start of the lesson, discuss the language used in formal and informal situations (such as speaking to a stranger and speaking to a friend) and ask the children to suggest words and phrases that might be used in each: for example, informal language might include the use of slang and dialect expressions whereas formal language should not. Lead the children to realise that the same people use formal and informal language, but in different situations.

Group discussion and interaction

In this section the children use talk to explore and share ideas, and they collaborate in shared activities, such as solving a problem. The children take different roles in groups: for example, acting as scribe.

Listen carefully... (page 28). As a follow-up activity, ask the children to put the same words into other sentences and to think of strategies to help them remember the problems with these words. During the plenary, ask the children to think of more examples of homographs (words that are spelled the same but have different meanings).

Let's have a party! (page 29). In this activity the children plan a party as a group, negotiating to reach decisions that they are all happy with. During the plenary, discuss the different types of language used by the children who took different roles. What were the similarities or differences between the roles?

Design an advertisement (page 30). The children may find it helpful to look at/listen to examples of radio, television and radio advertisements. If possible, provide perfume or aftershave bottles for use as props.

Poetry game: 1 and 2 (pages 31–32). If possible, arrange the children in mixed-ability groups, and ensure that all members of the group contribute. Stress that the group should make a joint decision as to whether an answer is correct or incorrect, and that where there is a disagreement, the appointed leader has the final say. The answer to the riddle on page 31 is 'envelope'.

Add an adjective (page 33). This activity focuses on the children developing roles such as leader, reporter, scribe and mentor. When adding adjectives to the sentences, the children should discuss the differences they are making to the meaning. Encourage the children to vary the order in which they take turns.

Book machine (page 34). In this activity the children have ten minutes in which to choose a book to talk about, allocate roles and complete a structured review of the book. Point out that they will need to work together and not argue or waste time. The completed sheets could be used as a means of recommending books to other readers or to assess whether the children understand aspects of story structure.

Advertisement survey (page 35). Here the children investigate features of advertisements from television, radio or magazines. They should discuss what they have discovered and talk about how these features persuade people to buy the product. During the plenary, focus on the most important aspects of working as a group. Also talk about the differences between advertisements on television, radio or in magazines. Since advertisements are based on assumptions that people interpret things in the same way, it will be useful to pull out any points that the children disagreed about.

A class newsletter: 1 and 2 (pages 36–37). These pages encourage the children to allocate roles in order to produce a class newsletter. Page 36 structures the activity through six stages – from planning to publication and launch. Page 37 provides guidance for planning and writing a newspaper article. ICT facilities will be useful to enable the children to produce professional results. It may be appropriate for you to select the key members of the group, but all children can be involved. The activity could form the basis of an extended role-play inside the office of a publisher, providing an opportunity for speaking and listening in a real-world context.

Bright ideas (page 38). Discuss with the class how the style of a presentation depends on its audience and purpose. Encourage them to notice presentational differences such as the use of stress, variation in the speed of delivery, tone of voice and use of gestures. If possible, provide Sellotape and Post-it notes for the children to use as visual aids in their presentations in the extension activity.

Speech success: 1 and 2 (pages 39–40). In this activity the children plan and present a group speech, and assess the speeches given by other groups. Page 39 assists the children in structuring a formal speech, particularly identifying which will be their most important points. Page 40 provides a chart which helps the audience to identify main points and evaluate how they are presented. For further work on body language, you could ask groups to role-play speeches where body language such as eye contact or excessive gesturing is evident, and ask for feedback on how the arguments were presented.

Drama

These activities provide useful and fun starting points to encourage a dramatic response and to allow the children to express themselves effectively – in role-play, when script-writing and when offering constructive criticism.

Costume design (page 41). When designing the costumes, the children should consider the intended audience as well as the period in which the story is set (13th century). Some research into medieval costume may be appropriate. Ensure that the children think about how to make the story exciting for younger children, and what kind of words the audience will understand.

Cinderella interview (page 42). Interviewing is a good role-play activity as it encourages the children to plan what to say in order to gain useful responses. You may wish to put a child in the 'hot seat' to answer questions from the class in role.

Mummification (page 43). You could record the children's role-plays and play them to the class during the plenary session. Ask the audience to comment on whether the process is explained clearly; whether the

'reporter' and 'expert' use their voices to make the programme interesting; and what else they could have done to create a better relationship with the audience.

Magic cat (page 44). The poem is a mysterious one so there is no correct answer to any of the questions: characters can be added or developed; the events are magical so not restricted to logic; the ending of the story is not obvious. The sheet gives four cues in the form of a writing frame so that the story can be developed before being made into a script. Point out that writing a good script involves the writer seeing and telling the story from the point of view of each character.

Alice meets Humpty Dumpty (page 45). Stress to the children that drama often uses a script, but that plays are intended to be watched rather than read. The director or the writer helps the actors to interpret their parts by providing stage directions. Sometimes these will tell the person on stage how to behave in order to achieve the required effect of characterisation or emotion; sometimes they simply tell the characters where to move on the stage. When the children have inserted stage directions into the script, they could compare their version with that of another pair, discussing the different ways in which the two scripts might be acted out.

The Pied Piper (page 46). This sheet provides the children with a section of a poem to discuss in groups. The language is vivid and the aim is for the children to use the descriptions to help them decide how characters in the story feel and how this varies between characters. The rats are characterised by the use of adjectives in the first section, and the rhythm of the poem gives a sense of their movement. The second section looks at the movement of the children as they follow the Piper.

What would I do? (page 47). This sheet provides a stimulus for thinking about possible actions and reactions when faced with a moral problem. Here, the group is provided with three questions to discuss, but others could be added. Again, it should be stressed that each contribution is valid as long as it is backed up by a suitable argument. Some children may think that the artwork shows a clear intention of theft, but their discussions may bring out the fact that the context is important. This will depend on exactly what the boy in the picture saw and whether he could be getting the wrong impression: for example, perhaps the girl is the daughter of the shopkeeper, or she is taking *out* of her pocket something she bought elsewhere.

How did you do? (page 48). This assessment sheet enables teachers and children to identify strengths and areas for improvement. The sheet is not intended for use after every activity, but should be given when it is felt appropriate. Sections not applicable to the activity can be masked.

Dog rules – OK!

- **Read the poem.**
- **Underline each rule in a different colour.**

Work as a group.

Rules for my dog

Don't sit under my chair when I'm
eating my dinner and make smells.
Everyone looks at me and says
'Stop it!' and it's not fair!

Don't keep putting your wet nose
in my pocket – my mouse doesn't like it.

Don't dig up Dad's best rose trees.
I don't need you to help me find
my worms.

Don't lick my knees.
It's horrible.
Go and lick my sister.

Geraldine Taylor

- **Discuss the rules:**

How many rules are there?

What reasons does the speaker give for each 'Don't …'

Which reason do you think is the best?

- **Were there any problems in making group decisions? What were they?**

Teachers' note Before the children start the activity, discuss why rules are important and talk about examples of situations in which rules are used. Then agree and list some ground rules for dialogue, such as taking turns and listening to others. When discussing the rules, make sure that all the children have a chance to contribute, so that the rules they devise are more meaningful to them.

Now try this!

- **With your group, make up four rules for a different pet.**

Developing Literacy
Speaking & Listening
Year 4
© A & C BLACK

Animal sort: 1

- **Talk about these animals. Discuss their similarities and differences.**
- **Use the chart on *Animal sort: 2* to sort the animals.**

Use the chart on *Animal sort: 2*

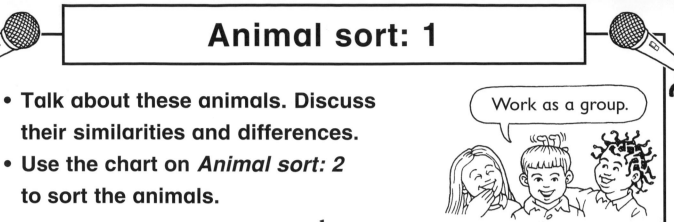

Work as a group.

frog

grasshopper

rabbit

eagle

fish

fox

salamander

snail

snake

ant

crane

deer

duck

Now try this!

- **With your group, find out which of the animals are** | insects | , | mammals | **and** | reptiles | .
- **In what ways are these three groups different?**

Teachers' note Use this with page 11. The children should decide as a group on different ways of sorting the animals, using the chart on page 11 as a starting point (they need not restrict themselves to the headings on the chart). If preferred, the children could work in pairs, reading out each heading on the chart and discussing which animals fit the description.

**Developing Literacy
Speaking & Listening
Year 4
© A & C BLACK**

Animal sort: 2

- **Write the animals in the correct places on the chart.**

Characteristics	
Six legs or more	Fewer than six legs
Long legs	Short legs
Lives on land	Lives in water
Has fur/feathers	No fur/feathers
Has antennae	No antennae
Visible tail	No tail

Teachers' note Use this with page 10. The children will need access to information books or the Internet to check their observations and find more information. Explain to the children that there may not always be a 'correct answer' and sometimes animals may not fit neatly into the chart (for example, frogs spend time both in water and on the land).

Developing Literacy Speaking & Listening Year 4 © A & C BLACK

School dinner discussions

Should school dinners be changed?

- **Complete the sentences to help you think about different points of view.**

Some people think that school dinners should be free because…	
I think that school dinners should be healthier because…	
My ideal school dinner would be…	
My worst school dinner would be…	
Children should not be able to eat what they want because…	
Not all children know why we need to eat balanced meals. They should be taught about…	

- **Use the sentences to discuss school dinners.**

Work as a group.

Now try this!

- **Cut out the sentences and shuffle them. Ask a partner to match up the parts of the sentences.**
- **Does your partner disagree with any of the points of view? Discuss why.**

Teachers' note Make sure that the children complete the sentences before they cut out the cards. You could use this opportunity to revise what makes a complete sentence (linking with sentence-level objectives).

**Developing Literacy
Speaking & Listening
Year 4
© A & C BLACK**

School dinner arguments

- **Think about the differences between a discussion and an argument. Tick the statements that are true.**

A In a discussion people talk and listen to others. ☐	**B** In an argument people respond to other people's views, stating their point of view. ☐	**C** In a discussion people only speak when spoken to. ☐	**D** In an argument people shout at each other. ☐

- **Argue against each point of view. Write two sentences.**

School dinners should be free – we need energy to keep working all day.

_____
_____
_____

People try to make school dinners too healthy, so dinners just end up being boring.

_____
_____
_____

Children know what is best for them – they should choose what they eat for lunch.

_____
_____
_____

Children should be made to eat school dinners – and everything on their plate.

_____
_____

Now try this!

- **Work with a partner. Choose one of the speech bubbles above.**
- **Role-play an argument. One of you should argue for the point of view. The other should argue against it.**

Think carefully about how you will do this without shouting or losing your temper.

Teachers' note Talk about the differences between a discussion and an argument before the children complete the activity sheet. Use the four statements at the top of the sheet as starting points. Stress that arguments are not about who shouts the loudest, but are about convincing others of your point of view through the use of persuasive language.

Developing Literacy
Speaking & Listening
Year 4
© A & C BLACK

Mapping journeys

- **Work as a group.**
- **Talk about what you know of the episodes in Jesus' life from his birth until his baptism.**

Why did Jesus have to move so much?

Who was with him?

Where in the Bible should we look?

Born in Bethlehem. He arrives in Jerusalem at 40 days old.

↓

His family take him to Egypt to escape Herod.

↓

Mary, Joseph and Jesus go home to Nazareth.

↓

At 12 years old, he goes with Mary and Joseph to Jerusalem for the Feast of Passover. Returns to Nazareth.

↓

He becomes a carpenter in Nazareth.

↓

As an adult, he travels to Bethany beyond the Jordan. He is baptised by John the Baptist in the River Jordan.

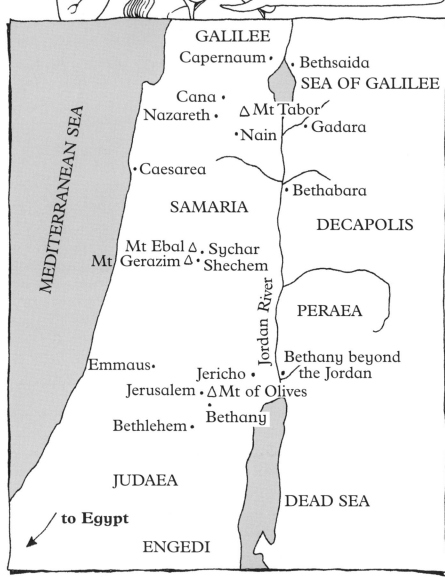

- **Draw arrows on the map to show the journeys. Use coloured pencils.**

- **Find out about the life of another religious leader, such as the Buddha or the prophet Muhammad.**
- **Talk about their journeys and what they did.**

Teachers' note The children should discuss the locations of the places mentioned and the possible routes of the journeys. Suggest that they draw the routes in pencil first so that they can adapt them if necessary in the light of discussion. They will need coloured pencils. When the groups have finished, they should present their maps and explain how they decided as a group where to draw the routes.

Developing Literacy Speaking & Listening Year 4 © A & C BLACK

Story maker

- **Use the cards from row A, B or C.**
- **Take turns to tell a story to your group.**
- **Discuss what was the same about the stories. How were they different?**

Work as a group.

	Setting	Character	Genre
A	castle	wizard	Fantasy
B	cottage	the Three Bears	Fairy tale
C	Sherwood Forest	Robin Hood	Legend

- **The others in your group should choose a 'wild card' from below. Talk about how this might change your story.**

computer   Valentine's Day card   space alien

Now try this!

- **Cut out the picture cards.**
- **Choose four cards and tell a story.**
- **Talk about how and why others have made their stories different.**

What happens when Robin Hood meets an alien and the Three Bears in a castle…?

Teachers' note It is important that the children are aware of the three genres on the page and can think of stories they have seen, read or heard that belong to each genre. Encourage the children to tell their stories clearly and logically and to respond to the suggestions of others in their group in appropriate ways.

Developing Literacy Speaking & Listening Year 4 © A & C BLACK

Soupy boy

Look! Is it a bird? Is it a plane?

NO! It's none of these! It's...

Here he is from closer up...

Tin can
Elbow
Flying cape
Leg

Youch! Careful with those arrows!
Cool 'Soupy Boy' logo
Other leg

"Gosh!" I hear you say. "Just who *is* this mysterious souper being?"
Well, make yourself comfortable and prepare to hear a tale which will ASTONISH and AMAZE!

Goo goo!   Ga ga!

Meet Ashley Fugg. Twelve years ago this cute baby had a TERRIBLE ACCIDENT...

From *The Amazing Adventures of Soupy Boy* by Damon Burnard

- **Make up the story of how Ashley Fugg became Soupy Boy.**

- **Tell the story to your group.**

- **Choose one of the stories told by a member of your group. Act it out.**

Teachers' note First allow time for the children to make up their stories, making notes and/or drawing quick pictures as prompts for their storytelling. Ensure that the children look carefully at the pictures on the activity sheet and use them as a basis for their stories. Then split the class into groups and give each child the opportunity to tell their story.

Developing Literacy
Speaking & Listening
Year 4
© A & C BLACK

Cartoon crazy

This cartoon has been put together in the wrong way.

- Cut out the pieces and put it together correctly.

- Take turns to tell the story. Think about how you will use your voice to make it interesting.

Tell the story to a partner.

- Ask your partner how they know which is the beginning , the middle and the end of the story.

Mr Croc Rocks!
by Frank Rodgers

Have I switched on? Yes.

Set the correct speed? Yes.

Turned up the volume? Yes!

So...let's go!

Oh no!

I've just remembered what it was I forgot.

I can't dance.

Mr Hound says this record is good to dance to.

So.. let's do it!

But before I do... there's something I'm sure I've forgotten.

Rock 'n Roll!

Oh yeh!

Oh...yeh?

Oh...oh!

Now try this!

- Make up your own cartoon strip about Mr Croc going to the swimming pool. Tell the story to your partner.
- Ask your partner which is the beginning, middle and end of the story. Do you both agree?

Teachers' note First revise simple story structure using a traditional fairy tale. Also discuss ways of telling a story effectively, such as using gestures and pausing for dramatic effect. You may wish to make an OHT of the page and talk about the cartoon with the whole class, before letting pairs or groups decide what the best order would be.

Developing Literacy
Speaking & Listening
Year 4
© A & C BLACK

Food chains

You are going to explain to your group how this food chain works.

 Use a dictionary.

SUN – original source of energy – light.

PLANT – takes light – makes food/energy – photosynthesis.

CARNIVORE – eats rabbit – takes in energy from food.

HERBIVORE – eats plant – takes in energy.

- **Make notes before you speak.**

Notes

- **Take turns to talk about the food chain.**

 Work as a group.

- **Find other examples of food chains. Discuss how they are similar to and different from the one above.**

Teachers' note Split the class into small groups and give each child a copy of this page so that they can make notes individually. The children could cut out the pictures and put them in a line if this helps them to see how the chain works. Remind the children that their notes do not need to be written in complete sentences. They will need access to information books about food chains.

**Developing Literacy
Speaking & Listening
Year 4
© A & C BLACK**

Good evening... and welcome

This TV presenter is interviewing a film star.

- **Read the clipboard and the speech bubbles. Label the speech bubbles to show the correct order.**

A Begin the interview.

B Start with a question to make the person feel comfortable.

C Begin to ask questions about the person's work.

D Continue to ask questions about their work.

E Signal the end of the interview.

> Well, that about wraps it up for this evening. ☐

> Let's move on to the next film in your career. ☐

> Perhaps you would like to tell the audience what you are doing in the country? ☐

> Welcome, and it's great to have you on the show. ☐

> So how did you get your first break in films? ☐

- **Work with a partner. Compare your answers. Discuss which words and phrases helped you to put the speech bubbles in the correct order.**

Now try this!

- **Try saying the speech bubbles in different ways to change the meaning.**
- **With your partner, role-play the interview using different tones of voice. How does this change the interview?**

> Suppose you don't like the person you are interviewing.

Teachers' note Before beginning, talk about the children's favourite television interviewers and the ways in which they speak. Do they speak formally or informally? Do they often ask the same kinds of questions? Model saying some of the speech bubbles in different ways to sound friendly/unfriendly or patient/impatient, and ask the children to comment on the effect.

Developing Literacy
Speaking & Listening
Year 4
© A & C BLACK

How does it make you feel?

- **Cut out the cards. Your teacher will play you a piece of music from a TV programme.**
- **Choose two cards which describe how it makes you feel.**
- **Explain to a partner why you chose these cards.**
- **On the blank cards, write three more** adjectives **to describe how the music makes you feel.**

sad	happy	frightened
calm	excited	angry
cheerful	sleepy	worried

Now try this!

- **Listen to the music from three other TV programmes.**
- **Talk to a partner about how the music makes you feel.**
- **Draw a chart to help you explain how you feel.**

Name of programme	The music makes me feel... because...	It makes me think about... because...

Teachers' note Play a video recording of a suitable extract from a television programme, such as the opening theme tune from a comedy programme. (You could change some of the words on the activity sheet to suit the music you have chosen.) Talk about the children's feelings and the reasons for them. For the extension activity, the children could watch the opening theme tunes of three soap operas.

Developing Literacy
Speaking & Listening
Year 4
© A & C BLACK

Television sight and sound

Work with a partner.

- Watch part of an information programme.
- What do you see and hear? Write about two different scenes.

Title

Scene (describe what you see)	Sounds (describe what you hear)		
	Narration	Music	Other sounds

- What difference would it make if you could not hear the sound? Find out and describe it.

Teachers' note Show two or more scenes from an information programme connected with any subject. With the whole class, discuss the images (which may include moving images, still photographs, drawings, diagrams and text), spoken words (narration), music (incidental music, theme music) and other sounds (including sound effects).

Developing Literacy
Speaking & Listening
Year 4
© A & C BLACK

Take pride

- **Read out this narration from a TV programme.**
- **Try using your voice in different ways.**

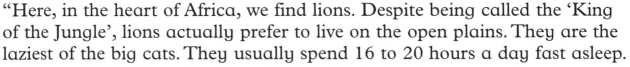

Work in a group. Take turns.

"Here, in the heart of Africa, we find lions. Despite being called the 'King of the Jungle', lions actually prefer to live on the open plains. They are the laziest of the big cats. They usually spend 16 to 20 hours a day fast asleep.

The male lion is easily recognised by his bushy brown mane and can weigh up to 250 kilograms. The females are much smaller, usually weighing in at no more than 180 kilograms. Adult lions usually have plain, golden fur. The cubs are marked with spots, which sometimes stay on their legs and their bellies until they are fully grown.

Lions live in family groups called prides. The females do the hunting for the pride, while the males defend the borders of their territory. A lion's roar can be heard up to 8 kilometres away, and up close it can be very frightening. In the wild, lions live for around 10 to 14 years, while in zoos they can live for over 20 years.

Pictures of lions have been found in stone-age cave paintings. They are also often seen in coats of arms, particularly in the United Kingdom where the lion is a national symbol of the British people. Today lions are a protected species in many countries. The majority of the world's lions are found in national parks in East and southern Africa."

- **Use your voice to make the narration sound:**
  - **(a)** serious
  - **(b)** light-hearted
  - **(c)** boring
  - **(d)** exciting

- **Talk with your group about how you made the narration sound different.**

Teachers' note At the start of the lesson, show the children extracts from television documentaries and discuss the qualities of the narrators' voices. Suggest to the children that one child in the group reads out the whole passage first. The others should comment on how the speaker uses his or her voice to make it interesting. Then the group should experiment with reading the passage in different ways.

Developing Literacy
Speaking & Listening
Year 4
© A & C BLACK

Getting stressed

The way you say something can change its meaning.

> **Who** ate my sweets?

> Who ate **my** sweets?

- **Work with a partner and take turns to have the sheet.**
- **Pick one of the sentences and read it aloud. Put the stress on the word in bold. Your partner should say which word was stressed and what the sentence means.**
- **Swap roles and repeat.**

> **He** broke my bike.

> He **broke** my bike.

> He broke **my** bike.

> He broke my **bike**.

throb!

Now try this!

- **With your partner, try saying this sentence in different ways.**

> A TV crew is interviewing my next-door neighbour.

Teachers' note Model the example first, stressing different words each time you read it. Talk about the different meanings created by placing stress on different words in the same sentence. For the extension activity, the children should listen to each other and discuss how the meaning of the sentence changes.

**Developing Literacy
Speaking & Listening
Year 4
© A & C BLACK**

All about kittens

Your teacher will role-play a vet who is visiting the school to talk about kittens.

• Listen carefully and make notes.

Notes

• **Answer the questions by discussing them and comparing your notes.**

Work as a group.

How old should a kitten be before it is taken from its mother?	
What should you look for when getting a kitten?	
Why does a kitten need many small meals?	
When will you see the real colour of your cat's eyes?	
How much more will your cat weigh when it is fully grown?	

Now try this!

• **Imagine you want to get a kitten. With a partner, role-play a conversation where you try to persuade your parent or carer. Use your notes.**

Teachers' note Give a talk about kittens, speaking in role as a vet (see page 7). You may need to read the passage twice to allow the children to make effective notes. In the extension activity, both children should use their notes as evidence to support their arguments for or against having a kitten.

Developing Literacy Speaking & Listening Year 4 © A & C BLACK

Plastic fun

A rain gauge and a mini-hothouse have been made from plastic bottles. You each have a picture of one of the objects.

Work with a partner.

- **Take turns to listen carefully as your partner describes his/her picture.**
- **Make notes and then draw the object.**

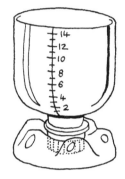

Rain gauge

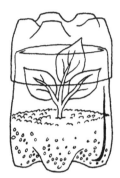

Mini-hothouse

Notes

Now try this!

- **Invent other ways of re-using plastic in schools.**
  Example: bottle tops could become Christmas decorations.

  fabric softener bottle top

- **Give a talk about how to make these things.**

Teachers' note For each pair, make one copy of the sheet with the picture of the rain gauge masked and another copy with the picture of the mini-hothouse masked. Stress that each child must keep their picture hidden. Briefly discuss the purpose of a rain gauge and a mini-hothouse before beginning. If possible, have available plastic bottles/bottle tops to help the children with the extension activity.

**Developing Literacy
Speaking & Listening
Year 4
© A & C BLACK**

Phone a friend

You overhear person X talking on a mobile phone.

> Hello… Fine… Did she really?… No… I don't believe it!…
> Yes… She won't come… See you later then… Bye.

- **Role-play the conversation with a partner. Make up what the person on the other end of the phone says (person Y).**
- **Now write what you think person Y might say.**

Hello.

Fine.

Did she really?

No.

I don't believe it!

Yes.

She won't come.

See you later then.

Bye.

Now try this!

- **Work in pairs to role-play more phone conversations.**

Teachers' note If possible, have available old phones for the role-plays. The children should first role-play the conversation as two friends talking. In the extension activity, they could role-play a conversation between two strangers and comment on how this is different. Also encourage pairs of children to listen to one another's conversations and discuss similarities and differences.

**Developing Literacy
Speaking & Listening
Year 4
© A & C BLACK**

26

Hello, goodbye

Here are some formal and informal ways of saying 'hello' and 'goodbye'.

Work with a partner.

• Cut out the cards.
• Put them in order, starting with the most formal.

Morning	Bye-bye
How are you?	Goodbye
Good morning	Cheerio
Hello	See you later
How do you do?	Farewell
Hi	Ta-ta for now
How's it going?	Bye
Long time, no see	Good evening

Now try this!

• Role-play two conversations: one formal and one informal. How are they different?

Hello, hello, hello!

Teachers' note Give each pair one copy of this page. Before starting the activity, check that the children understand the meaning of 'formal' and 'informal'. Discuss situations when formal and informal language is appropriate (for example, with the headteacher/in the playground).

Developing Literacy
Speaking & Listening
Year 4
© A & C BLACK

Listen carefully...

- **Work as a group. Decide who will do what.**
- **Someone should cut out the cards.**
- **One person chooses a card and reads it out.**
- **Someone else says which words they think sound different but are spelled the same.**
- **Choose someone to write the spellings and the meanings of the words.**

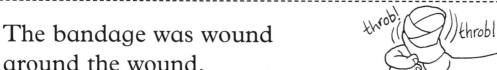

Use a dictionary.

The bandage was wound around the wound.

The farm was used to produce produce.

The dump was so full that it had to refuse more refuse.

The soldier decided to desert his dessert in the desert.

There was a row among the oarsmen about how to row.

The tear in the painting made her shed a tear.

Now try this!

- **In your group, re-write the sentences. Use words that are all spelled differently.**

Teachers' note You may need to use only a few of the examples, depending on the ability of the groups. Encourage the children to think about how they will decide who will take which roles in the group (the leader, the scribe, the reader, the person who does the cutting out). Will the same children do the same task throughout the activity, or will they swap roles?

Developing Literacy Speaking & Listening Year 4 © A & C BLACK

Let's have a party!

- **Plan a party. Decide who is going to organise the guest list, the food and drink, games and music.**
- **Each person should list their ideas.**

My list

- **As a group, decide on the final guest list, food, drink, and so on. Complete the lists.**

 Work as a group.

We would invite…

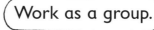

We would eat and drink…

We would play games such as…

Music we would listen to…

- **Now plan a party for your teacher. Which roles do you need in your group now?**

Teachers' note Each child will need one copy of this page. Begin by discussing the tasks that are required to organise a party. Encourage the children to think about how they can share out the tasks fairly. Each child plans a different aspect of the party, and writes a list of ideas. Then as a group, the children should take it in turns to explain their ideas and the group should negotiate the final lists.

Developing Literacy
Speaking & Listening
Year 4
© A & C BLACK

Design an advertisement

- **Work as a group.**
  You are going to design
  an advertisement for
  a new fragrance.
- **First decide on a name.**

What tasks do we have to carry out?

Who will do what?

Is it for TV, radio or magazines?

List words to describe the fragrance. ☐

Describe the setting of the advertisement. ☐

Name of fragrance:

_____

_____

_____

_____

_____

_____

_____

_____

What are you trying to make people believe? ☐

How will the advertisement appeal to the audience? ☐

Now try this!

- **As a group, work out how to make people want**
  to buy your fragrance. Design your advertisement.
- **Test your advertisement and ask for feedback.**

Teachers' note The children should work in groups of four, and between them allocate roles for working on different aspects of the advertisement. They will each need a copy of the sheet and should tick the task that they have carried out. Encourage them first to discuss and decide whom the product is aimed at. The finished advertisements could be displayed or performed for the class to discuss.

Developing Literacy
Speaking & Listening
Year 4
© A & C BLACK

Poetry game: 1

You need the cards from *Poetry game: 2*, two counters and a dice.

- **Pick two people to play.**
- **Decide who will have the final say if you have a disagreement.**

> Work as a group. Swap roles after every game.

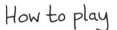

How to play

☆ Take turns to roll the dice.

☆ If you land on a 'Card' square, your partner picks a card and reads it to you.

☆ The group should discuss your answer. If they think it is **correct**, move on a square. If they think it is **incorrect**, miss a turn.

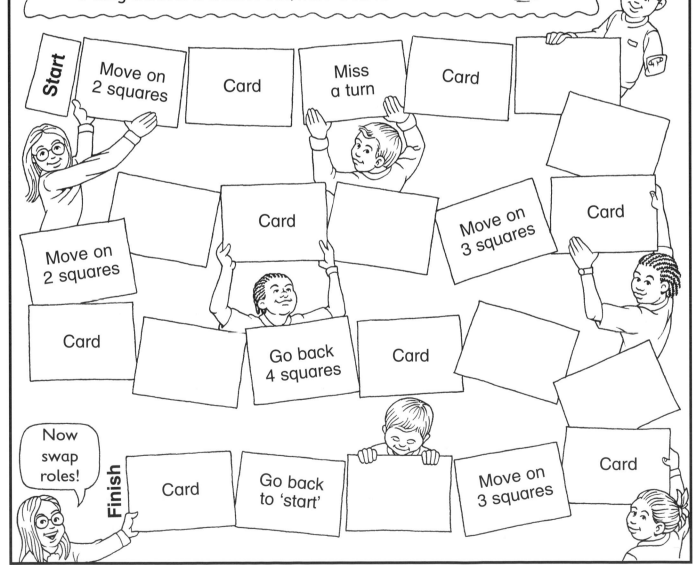

Start | Move on 2 squares | Card | Miss a turn | Card

Move on 2 squares | Card

Card | Card | Move on 3 squares | Card

Move on 2 squares | Card | Go back 4 squares | Card

Now swap roles! | **Finish** | Card | Go back to 'start' | Move on 3 squares | Card

Teachers' note Use this with page 31 (each group needs one copy of each page). All group members should be involved in discussing the answers. Some questions are quite open and there may be more than one correct answer; the group should decide whether the answer given is good enough for the player to move on. During the plenary, discuss the game and resolve any disagreements.

Developing Literacy Speaking & Listening Year 4 © A & C BLACK

Poetry game: 2

Which word is an example of onomatopoeia (a sound word)?
  A swing
  B swish
  C hit

A couplet has:
  A two lines
  B three lines
  C four lines

Say this without making a mistake.

'Swan swam over the sea. Swim, swan, swim.'

What rhymes with 'orange'?

Trick question – nothing rhymes with 'orange'. Move on a square!

Complete this simile.

'She's got a runny nose like a fireman's _____'

Where would you find an epitaph?
  A on a window
  B in a supermarket
  C on a gravestone

Complete this metaphor.

'The fog is a hungry ___ Licking at the windows.'

'Twinkle twinkle little bat! How I wonder what you're at!'

What was the original rhyme?

Say five words that rhyme with 'cat'.

How many syllables does a haiku have?
  A 17
  B 15
  C 12

What does this Cockney rhyming slang mean?

'apples and pears'

What is the missing word?

'Monday's child is fair of face.
Tuesday's child is full of _____'

What rhymes with 'silver'?

Trick question – nothing rhymes with 'silver'. Move on two squares!

A cinquain has:
  A five lines
  B four lines
  C three lines

What does this Cockney rhyming slang mean?

'north and south'

Complete this simile.

'As dry as a _____ As hard as a stone'.

Guess the riddle:

'Which eight-letter word contains only one letter?'

Which of these is the first line of a limerick?
  A 'Shall I compare thee to a summer's day?'
  B 'There was an old lady of Kent.'

Teachers' note Use this with page 31. The cards should be cut out and placed in a pile, face down.

**Developing Literacy
Speaking & Listening
Year 4
© A & C BLACK**

Add an adjective

- **Take turns to add an** `adjective` **to each sentence.**
- **Discuss how each adjective changes the character or object.**
One person should write down the new sentences.
Someone else should make notes about your discussions.

Work as a group.

> The princess is kissing a toad.
> The **young** princess is kissing a toad.
> The **young** princess is kissing a **slimy** toad.
> The **young, ugly** princess is kissing a **slimy** toad.
> The **young, ugly** princess is kissing a **slimy, unhappy** toad…

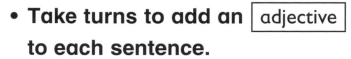

The dragon followed the wizard.

_____

_____

_____

_____

Our group won the trophy.

_____

_____

_____

_____

The dog ate my dinner.

_____

_____

_____

_____

Now try this!

- **Talk to the class about the adjectives your group chose.**

Teachers' note Split the class into groups of four and give each group a copy of this page. First revise adjectives and nouns. Using the examples on the page, draw out how the use of descriptive words can change meaning. Talk about how the roles of leader, reporter, scribe and mentor can be useful in group discussion. Each group should nominate a spokesperson for the extension activity.

Developing Literacy
Speaking & Listening
Year 4
© A & C BLACK

Book machine

- **Work as a group. Decide who will do what.**
- **Choose a book you have all read. Record your opinions on the machine. You have only 10 minutes!**

Title of book:	
Author:	
Draw favourite scene	**Draw favourite character**

Draw pointers to show how interesting it was. 10 = fabulous 1 = boring

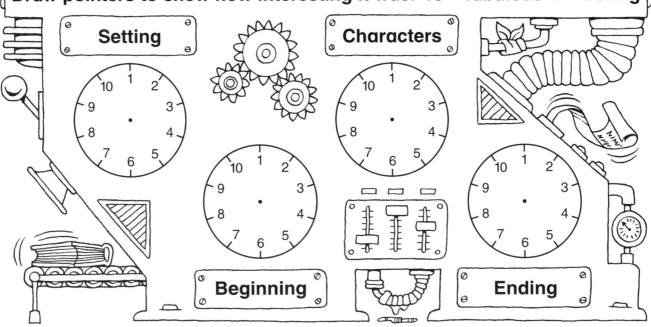

- **Now talk about what it was like to work as a group.**

  What went well? What did you find difficult?

Now try this!

- **Write a report about working in your group.**

  Who will write? Who will draw the pictures?

Teachers' note The group should decide on a book that they like and then consider the various aspects of it. They will need to choose a scribe, an illustrator and someone to keep track of time. After making joint decisions about each section, the appointed scribe/illustrator completes the form. During the plenary, a spokesperson could use the form to report back to the rest of the class.

Developing Literacy
Speaking & Listening
Year 4
© A & C BLACK

Advertisement survey

The cards below show some features of advertisements.

- **Work in a group of three.**
- **Cut out the cards. Use them to help you collect information about adverts.**

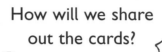

Where will we look: magazines, TV, radio?

How will we share out the cards?

How will we record our findings?

Settings to suggest a happy family life	Pictures to suggest good looks in men and women
Settings to suggest luxury	Words to suggest that you will be popular if you buy the product
Words to do with science	Words that sound technical
Mention of 'NEW'	Anything funny or a joke
Babies in adverts	Animals in adverts
Celebrities in adverts	Adjectives used to describe the product

- **Discuss with your group why adverts have these features.**

Now try this!

- **As a group, discuss which adverts you think work best.**
- **Present your findings to the class.**

Teachers' note The children will need access to magazines and recordings of television and radio advertisements. Set a time limit for the activity. Instead of using all the cards, you could divide them among various groups and then come together in the plenary to discuss them all. Encourage the children to evaluate their teamwork.

**Developing Literacy
Speaking & Listening
Year 4
© A & C BLACK**

A class newsletter: 1

- **Use this sheet to help you produce a class newsletter.**

Work as a group. Decide who will do what.

Name of newsletter: _____

Class: _____

Editor: _____

Writers: _____

Artists: _____

Stage 1: planning
- ◆ What type of newsletter?
- ◆ How many pages?
- ◆ What kind of articles?
  Who will write them?
  Who will illustrate them?

Stage 4: contents
- ◆ Which articles will be used?
- ◆ Cover design?
- ◆ Order of contents?
- ◆ Typesize?

Stage 2: drafting
- ◆ Talk to each other and start to get ideas for your articles down on paper.
- ◆ Pictures? Colour? Type of drawing?

Stage 5: final copy
- ◆ Proofreading needed?
- ◆ Are you happy with the cover?
- ◆ Are the pages numbered?
- ◆ How is it to be printed?
- ◆ How many copies?

Stage 3: editing
- ◆ Swap articles and suggest ways of improving them.
- ◆ Use a computer at this stage to present your articles.

Stage 6: launch
- ◆ How will you launch it – a party?
- ◆ Will you advertise the newsletter?
- ◆ How will you distribute it?
- ◆ Feedback – who enjoyed it?

Now try this!

- **Discuss how well you worked as a group.**
  How did you make decisions?
  What happened when you disagreed?

Teachers' note Use this in conjunction with page 37. Monitor the group closely during this activity, encouraging the children to use their time effectively and making sure tasks are completed. Encourage them to make back-up plans: for example, what will they do if printing in colour proves too expensive or if they cannot make as many copies as they would like?

**Developing Literacy
Speaking & Listening
Year 4
© A & C BLACK**

- **Work as a group.**
- **Read this unusual newspaper article.**
- **Plan and write your own article about something silly, strange or unusual happening in your classroom.**

> Who will plan it?

> Who will write it?

> Who will check it?

> How will we decide who will do which task?

> How will we decide what the article is about?

Horror as John's pen plunges from desk

Yesterday at an inner-city primary school, there was confusion and shock when a pen plunged from a desk and hit the floor.

The pen, a new blue ink-pen especially purchased for school by his 80-year-old grandmother, belonged to golden-haired John Smith – a year 4 pupil at Stonard Primary school in London's Docklands area – and is now totally useless.

Vanished from sight

When interviewed John said, 'It happened at about ten to two. I was just starting to think about my English work so I looked for my new pen. It had completely disappeared.'

Dan blames the girls

His friend Dan – a lively dark-haired sporty-type, also in year 4 – told us in confidence that he thought the girl at the next table must have deliberately wobbled the desk so the new pen fell.

John's teacher, Mr Barton (32 and slightly balding), said that he was looking into the matter and held up the pen with bent nib for us to see. The class were still in a state of shock about such a terrible event.

Now try this!

- **Write a report on working as a team.**

Teachers' note Use this in conjunction with page 36. Before the children begin, discuss the roles that will be needed to produce an article for a newsletter. Draw out the features of reports and explain that the children can make up a humorous incident if they wish. The extension activity can be carried out once the whole newsletter has been completed.

**Developing Literacy
Speaking & Listening
Year 4
© A & C BLACK**

Bright ideas

You are each going to give a presentation on an invention. Below are your notes.

Work as a group.

• **Choose a set of notes. Identify the most important points.**

• **Give a two-minute presentation to the rest of your group.**

The safety pin
Invented by Walter Hunt in 1849, USA – he played with a piece of wire. The clever thing about the pin is that the point fits into the clasp – stops it sticking into you, and stops it coming undone. He sold the idea for $400.

Blue denim jeans
Invented by Levi Strauss in 1873 – made from tough cotton called 'serge de Nimes' (the city in France where the cotton came from) – which gave us the word 'denim'. Jeans were meant for miners and cowboys – tough – used metal rivets.

The microwave oven
Invented by Percy Spencer in 1946 – a scientist – worked with a machine called a 'magnatron' (a device to produce short radio signals) – he walked past it and found that the bar of chocolate in his pocket had melted – realised the radio waves (microwaves) made heat. He used the idea to design an oven.

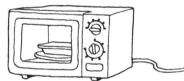

Frozen food
Invented (well… sort of) by Clarence Birdseye in 1923. He realised that you could stop food going off by freezing it. But many foods became tough if frozen – and vegetables became mushy and tasteless. He solved this problem by freezing food very quickly.

Now try this!

• **Split your group into two teams.**

• **Find out how** Sellotape **and** Post-it notes **were invented. Each team prepares and gives a presentation on one invention.**

• **What was similar or different about the presentations?**

Teachers' note The children should work in groups of four. Each child will need a copy of the sheet. Stopwatches will also be useful. You may need to read the notes to the children and explain anything that they do not understand. Discuss methods of selecting key facts, such as underlining or asking key questions. For the extension activity, the children will need access to the Internet.

Developing Literacy
Speaking & Listening
Year 4
© A & C BLACK

Speech success: 1

- **Use this sheet to help your group plan a four-minute speech on either:**

Work as a group.

Why we think we should have school uniform.

or

Why we think we should <u>not</u> have school uniform.

A Choose your argument:

B Write eight points to support your argument.

-
-
-
-
-
-
-
-

C Choose the six points you think are the best. Write them in order.

1.
2.
3.
4.
5.
6.

D Give more detail to each of your six points.

1.
2.
3.
4.
5.
6.

E Each write your own part of the speech onto cards to help you when you speak.

Now try this!

- **As a group, practise your four-minute speech.**
- **Can you think of ways to make it better?**

Use a stopwatch to time it.

Teachers' note The children should work in groups of four, completing sections A to D as a group and then writing their own part of the speech onto cards (section E). Each group will need a stopwatch. Encourage them to think about how they will present their ideas as well as the words they will use. The prepared speeches should be given to the class and assessed using the chart on page 40.

**Developing Literacy
Speaking & Listening
Year 4
© A & C BLACK**

Speech success: 2

- **Use this sheet to help you evaluate a group speech.**

Argument _____

Name of speaker				
How well did the speaker use notes?				
Did the speaker make eye contact with the audience?				
How clear was the speaking?				
What were the main points?				
How well were the ideas organised?				
Was the speech persuasive?				

- **As a group, compare the different speakers' arguments.**

- **Choose a spokesperson to tell the rest of the class what makes a good speech.**

Teachers' note Use this in conjunction with page 39. Before the speech is given, read through the questions on the chart with the children. Ask them to evaluate the speech as a group, but with each child making notes on their own copy of the sheet. Parts of the sheet could be masked and new features added.

Developing Literacy
Speaking & Listening
Year 4
© A & C BLACK

Costume design

- **Work as a group. You are going to perform a puppet play of** *The Pied Piper of Hamelin* **for younger children.**
- **Draw costumes on these characters. Cut them out and make stick puppets.**
- **Write a playscript. Keep the words simple.**
- **Perform your play for another group. Ask them to comment on your performance.**

child

child

child

rat

rat

rat

piper

mayor

rat

- **Now you have watched other groups, how would you change your play?**

Teachers' note Ensure that the children are familiar with the story of *The Pied Piper of Hamelin* (see page 46). The focus of this activity should be on groups commenting on others' performances, which should include evaluating the costumes and saying whether the play was suitable for young children. Provide resources for making the puppets, such as lollipop sticks.

**Developing Literacy
Speaking & Listening
Year 4
© A & C BLACK**

Cinderella interview

- **Imagine that you are going to interview Cinderella after her marriage to Prince Charming. What will you ask?**

Work with a partner.

- **Here are some questions. Together, write some more.**

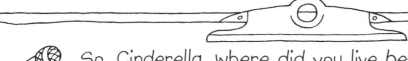

So, Cinderella, where did you live before you were married?

I heard that you had a pretty tough life. Perhaps you would like to tell us about this?

What changed all this?

And what did you think of all this magic?

- **Role-play the interview.**

- **Then write a script based on your role-play.**

Now try this!

- **Choose another traditional story character.**

What questions would you ask?

How would you ask them?

How might the character react?

- **Role-play the interview.**

- **Swap roles and choose a different character.**

Teachers' note Ensure that the children know the difference between open and closed questions. Model answering the questions on the activity sheet to show how they develop the conversation and do not 'close' it. Draw out that the interview would be very short if all the responses were simply 'yes' and 'no'!

**Developing Literacy
Speaking & Listening
Year 4
© A & C BLACK**

Mummification

- **Work with a partner. Imagine you are making a radio programme. One of you is a reporter and the other is a mummy expert. The reporter should ask questions that will help the expert explain how to make mummies.**
- **Use the diagrams and the notes to help you role-play the radio programme.**

Remove organs – brain was hooked out of nose – rest removed through cuts in side – organs stored in jars (canopic jars).

Drying – body covered in special salt (natron) took a month to dry out – could not decompose.

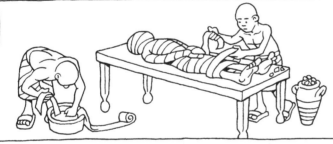

Wrapping – strips of linen wrapped around body – special jewels (believed to have magic properties) woven in with bandages.

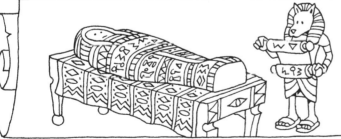

Entombing – mummy encased special papyrus (Book of the Dead) placed with it – mummy placed inside special wooden or metal sarcophagus – buried in tomb.

- **Together, write up your role-play into a script.**

- **Find out about one of these ancient Egyptian topics:**
  gods and goddesses   building pyramids
- **Write a script for another radio programme.**

Teachers' note If possible, play a radio interview at the start of the lesson and discuss how a radio interview differs from one on television. Before the children begin the activity, ask them what they already know about mummification in ancient Egypt. For the extension activity, ensure the children have access to other history resources on ancient Egypt.

**Developing Literacy
Speaking & Listening
Year 4
© A & C BLACK**

Magic cat

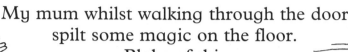

- **Read the poem.**

Work with a partner.

Magic cat

My mum whilst walking through the door
spilt some magic on the floor.
Blobs of this
and splots of that
but most of it upon the cat.

Our cat turned magic, straight away
and in the garden went to play
where it grew two massive wings
and flew around in fancy rings ...

Peter Dixon

- **Write a playscript about what happens now that the cat is magic. First make notes on the chart below. Think about how the characters feel, and what they will say and do.**

Why does Mum spill the magic?	How does the cat feel about being magic?
How does Mum feel about the cat being magic?	What other magical changes might happen to the cat? How will the characters react?

- **Perform your play to the rest of the class.**
- **How did other children answer the questions on the chart? What did you think of their plays?**

Teachers' note Talk about the structure of the poem and its rhymes, as well as the content. Invite the children to fill in the background to the poem and suggest what might happen, but stress that there is no 'right answer'. The children should work in pairs to generate ideas and improvise scenes before writing their playscript.

**Developing Literacy
Speaking & Listening
Year 4**
© A & C BLACK

Alice meets Humpty Dumpty

- **Write stage directions for this script. Show what Alice is like and why she acts as she does. The first one is done for you.**

> Work with a partner.

Alice is in the mysterious land through the mirror. She is surprised to see Humpty Dumpty sitting very still on a narrow wall in front of her. He does not take any notice of her.

Alice: (whispering to herself)
He is very like an egg. I would recognise him anywhere.

Humpty Dumpty:
It is very provoking to be called an egg. Very!

Alice: _____
I said you looked like an egg, Sir. And some are very pretty you know.

Humpty Dumpty:
Some people have no more sense than a baby.

Alice: _____
Humpty Dumpty sat on a wall,
Humpty Dumpty had a great fall…

Humpty Dumpty:
The last line is much too long for the poetry. Don't stand chattering to yourself like that. Tell me your name and your business.

Alice: _____
My name is Alice, but…

Humpty Dumpty:
It's a stupid name. What does it mean?

Alice: _____
Must a name mean something?

Humpty Dumpty:
Of course it must. My name means the shape I am – and a good, handsome shape it is. With a name like yours, you might be any shape almost.

Alice: _____
Why do you sit out here all alone?

- **Now think about the discussion from Humpty's point of view. Add in stage directions for him.**

Teachers' note You may need to read the text with the children and model the use of stage directions. Talk about what the children already know about Alice and Humpty Dumpty. As a further extension, the pairs could continue the script, remembering to include stage directions, and perform the play for another pair.

**Developing Literacy
Speaking & Listening
Year 4
© A & C BLACK**

45

The Pied Piper

• **Read the poem together.**

Work as a group.

… And out of the houses the rats came tumbling.
Great rats, small rats, lean rats, brawny rats,
Brown rats, black rats, grey rats, tawny rats…
Brothers, sisters, husbands, wives –
Followed the Piper for their lives.
From street to street he piped advancing,
And step for step they followed dancing…

Once more he stepped into the street;
And to his lips again
Laid his long pipe of smooth straight cane;
And ere he blew three notes (such sweet
Soft notes as yet magician's cunning
Never gave the enraptured air)
There was a rustling, that seemed like a bustling
Of merry crowds justling at pitching and hustling,
Small feet were pattering, wooden shoes clattering,
Little hands clapping and little tongues chattering…

Out came the children running.
All the little boys and girls,
With rosy cheeks and flaxen curls,
And sparkling eyes and teeth like pearls,
Tripping and skipping, ran merrily after
The wonderful music with shouting and laughter.

From *The Pied Piper of Hamelin* by Robert Browning

• **Now split into two groups (the Rats and the Children).**

Rats discuss these questions:

How do you think the townspeople feel about the rats following the Pied Piper? How do the rats feel?

• **Children discuss these questions:**

How do you think the townspeople feel about the children following the Pied Piper? How do the children feel?

• **Choose someone to be the Pied Piper. Half of the Rats and half of the Children are now townspeople.**

• **Act out the story. Remember what you have discussed about how the different characters feel.**

Teachers' note Ensure that the children are familiar with the story of *The Pied Piper of Hamelin*. Explain how the townspeople asked the Piper to rid the town of rats but refused to pay him the full amount that they had promised. Read the poem extract to the children and help them with any difficult language. Encourage the children to annotate the poem by underlining or circling key words.

**Developing Literacy
Speaking & Listening
Year 4
© A & C BLACK**

What would I do?

• **Work as a group. Discuss what is happening in the picture.**

• **Imagine you are the boy in the picture. Take turns to role-play what he would say about how he felt and what he should do. Use the questions to help you.**

What did I feel about this?

Who would I tell and why?

What would I do straight away?

• **Imagine you are the girl in the picture. Role-play what she would say about why she was doing this if someone asked her.**

Teachers' note There is no 'right answer' here, but encourage the children to consider the moral issues of 'right' and 'wrong' (link this with similar themes in PSHE). It is important for the children to discuss why someone would do such a thing in the first place.

Developing Literacy Speaking & Listening Year 4 © A & C BLACK

How did you do?

Name _____ Date _____

Activity title _____

> **When you listened to others**

- **What was good about what they said?**

  _____

  _____

- **What could they have done better?**

  _____

  _____

> **When you spoke**

- **What did you do well?**

  _____

  _____

- **What could you do better next time?**

  _____

  _____

> **When you talked in a group**

- **What was good about your discussion?**

  _____

  _____

- **Did you have any problems? If you did, what were they?**

  _____

  _____

Teachers' note Photocopy this page and fill in the title of the activity to be self-assessed. Before the children complete the assessment sheet, you could ask them whether they enjoyed the activity, and to explain why or why not.

**Developing Literacy
Speaking & Listening
Year 4**
© A & C BLACK